Heavenly Citizen Little Lights
Series

Shine Your Heavenly Light

HEAVENLY CITIZEN

By

Gabriel & **A**ngélique Marcelin

Heavenly Citizen: **Little Lights Series**
Copyright © 2025 by:
Gabriel & Angelique Marcelin
All rights reserved.

No part of this book may be reproduced,
stored in a retrieval system,
or transmitted in any form or by any means,
electronic, mechanical,
photocopying, recording, or otherwise,
without prior written permission
from the publisher, except for brief
quotations used in reviews,
articles, or educational materials.

Published by Heavenly Citizen Publishing
www.HeavenlyCitizen.shop

All illustrations, images, and designs are the
exclusive property of the authors and are
protected under international copyright
laws.

Scripture quotations, unless otherwise
noted, are from the Holy Bible.

This book is a story of love, created for
children and their families.
Any resemblance to actual persons is
coincidental and unintentional.

ISBN: 978-1-0696534-8-2 (Hardcover)
ISBN: 978-1-0696534-9-9 (Paperback)
Printed in Canada / United States

DEDICATION

To our precious boys
Gabe Jr., Isaiah, and Gershom Marcelin
You are our gifts from God, the blessings
we cherish every day.
May your lives always be filled with joy,
faith, and the gentle light of Jesus.

May this book remind you of who you truly
are: children of God, beloved by Christ.
Wonderfully made, and chosen with
purpose. May you shine His heavenly light
and brighten the world with your kindness
and love.

To:
Every child and **every family** reading these
Christian inspirational words from **heaven**,
this book is for you. The little **Heavenly
Citizens, LITTLE LIGHTS** shining with love,
faith, and purpose over your child and your
homes.

May this book and its stories fill your hearts
with joy, wisdom, and the light of Jesus.
And may everyone in your family become a
reader, growing together in knowledge,
kindness, and heavenly understanding.

TABLE OF CONTENTS

HEAVENLY CITIZEN

Heavenly Citizen – Little Lights Series

1. Title: *Heavenly Citizen Little Lights Series* 1
2. Copyright 2
3. Dedication 3
4. Jesus Holding the Book of Life 5
5. God Created Everything 6
6. Children Are the Light of the World 7
8. Helping Others 8
9. My Mom Is a Poet 11
11. My Blessing Heroes 12
13. I Am a Child of God 12
14. The Meaning of "Light of the World" 14
15. Christmas: The Holiday of Love 15
16. The Heavenly Lights: Daddy Reads 16
17. Every Day Is a New Day 18
18. My Love Poem to Mommy and Daddy 19
19. Grandparents Are a Blessing 21
20. What Is the White House? 22
21. What Is Your Talent? 23
22. Country vs. Continent — What's the Difference? 22
23. The Doctors at Home 25
24. Don't Speak to Strangers 26
25. The Meaning of Your Name 27
26. I Am a Reader — Are You Too? 28
27. Do You Know Who Jesus Is? 29
31. Thank You, Friends — From Gershom 31

God made the sun, the stars, the skies,
Then placed a light inside your eyes.
A light of love, so pure, so true
A piece of heaven lives in you.

Matthew 5:14

Dear Jesus, help my light to shine,
in love, in joy, in every time.

Matthew 5:14
«You are the light that gives light to the world.
A city that is built on a hill cannot be hidden.»

Hello friends

My name is Gershom, what is your name?
My name is ....!
Great, I'm very happy to meet you.
When you help a friend who fell,
Your light rings bright like heaven's bell.
Jesus said:
«Help each other with your troubles.
When you do this, you truly obey the law of heaven.»

Galatians 6:2

My Mom Is a Poet

My mom is a poet …. she reads Maya Angelou.
Do you know what poetry is?
Let me share one with you.

....

Today is a good and blessed day
All of God's children smile and play.
Lovely songs and shining gifts on Christmas Day
Families laugh and friends all pray
Teachers clap as candles sway
We cut the cake and shout «Hooray!»
We bought our tickets; the crowd will cheer all day
The basketball finals are finally here today!

So many moments, bright and true birthday
My mom says poetry is seeing God in all we do every day
Every rhyme, every line, each joyful way,

My Blessing Heroes

My dad and my mom are my heroes.
They teach how to pray every day
Do you know how to pray?
Don't worry …. we can pray together!

Dear Heavenly Father,
Your light shines strong in every way.

Jehovah Rapha,
You are the greatest doctor and healer.
Please bring peace, joy, and strength
to every home and family,
Thank You for all moms and dads,
for their love and care each day.
In the name of Jesus, Amen.

I Am a Child of God

I respect myself.
God made me special, inside and out.
That's why I take good care of my body every day.

When I wake up in the morning, I brush my teeth, take a nice shower, and get ready for a brand-new day that God has made.

I listen to my parents because they love me and teach me what is right. They remind me that true beauty comes from a clean heart and a kind spirit.

When I dress, I choose clothes that make me look neat and respectful.

Being modest and heavenly citizen who light the whole world. »

HEAVENLY CITIZEN CHILDREN

I Am Smart

Say that with me « I am Smart »
I always do my best and shine bright at school, because I am a friend of Jesus.

My mom says all of God's children can do *all things* when we pray.

Say that with me « I am Smart »

Philippians 4:13
« *I can do all things through Christ who gives me strength.* »

The Lord made me intelligent and brave.
« **The Lord is my light and my salvation— whom shall I fear?** »
–*Psalm 27:1*

TIANJIN BINHAI LIBRARY (CHINA)

My Homework Is My Job

Daddy always says,
 My homework is my job.

That means God wants me to learn, grow and use my mind to solve problems.

When I study, I do my best to get 100% because God loves a cheerful learner!

Even when it's hard, I try again.
Mommy says every new thing I learn will make me more intligent.

Whatever you do, work,
I smile and remember
I'm working, and this is mjob.

What Does It Mean When Jesus Said, "You Are the Light of the World"?

(Matthew 5:14)

When Jesus said, "You are the light of the world." He was giving every child a special identity filled with goodness, kindness, and faith. Light is everything that is pure and Holy, and it always shows the presence of God.

King David said: « The Lord is my light and my salvation » (Psalm 27:1).

Jesus also said: « I am the light of the world. »

Let's say it together:
« I am the light of the world. »

Christmas
The Holiday of Love and Light

Christmas is our favorite season of light,
a time of joy, a happy season bright.
We sing, we smile, we pray with hearts so light,
for God is love, and God is light.
(1 John 4:8)

Songs fill the air, and the stars shine bright
every child's heart feels warm with delight.
"We love because He first loved us." What a sight!
That's what the Bible teaches is right.

Jesus was born to bring us light
a gift of joy far beyond any height.
So we share, we give, we pray each night
Thank You, God, for Christmas, pure and bright!

Merry Christmas to you all, may
your homes be filled with light.

The Heavenly Lights
Daddy Reads

Daddy sat with his children and said,

"Let me tell you something beautiful."

"There is a heavenly light that shines for every child.

God sends His Angels to guide you, protect you, and help your hearts shine with love."

Psalm 91:11

Dear God,
help my light shine today, and every day.

Bless every child in the world with peace, joy, and heavenly love.

Then Daddy gently whispered:
"Learn to say thank you for kindness and good manners, and sorry when we are wrong.

In Jesus' name, Amen.

My Love Poem to Mommy a Daddy

Dear Mommy and Daddy,
this is your little baby speaking.
I have so many words inside my heart—
heaven knows them all—
words of love, gratitude,
and joy because of you.

Before my first breath
you already knew me.
You chose a name filled with
blessing, a Christian name
with meaning and light.
For 9 months,
for 270 days,
6,480 hours,
388,800 minutes,
ou waited for me
with hope, patience,
and so much love.

I thank God
for choosing you to be my parents.
No words will ever be enough
to express haw much I love you.

I am proud to tél
the whole world:
with my soul

Love from Gershom and Olivia

ALL HEAVENLY LIGHTS LITTLE LIGHTS CHILDREN ARE CANDIDATES TO BE PRESIDENT ONE DAY

WHAT IS THE WHITE HOUSE?

The White House is a very special place. It is the home and workplace of the President of the United States. People all around the world recognize it because it is one of the most important buildings in America.

FUN FACTS ABOUT THE WHITE HOUSE

- It has 132 rooms inside!
- The first president to live there was. John Adams in 1800.
- It is always kept safe by the Secret Service

WHERE IS IT?

The White House is located at:
1600 Pennsylvania Avenue NW.
Washington, D.C..

What is your talent?
Let's ask the Lord Jesus Christ together.

"God gives everyone different talents. Some have many, some have a few, but all are important and meant to be used!"

Matthew 25:14–15

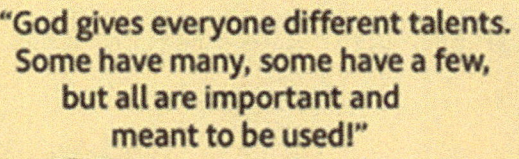

A Prayer for My Gifts and Talents

Dear Jesus,
Thank You for making me special.
Thank You for the gifts and talents
You put inside my heart.
Please help me discover them
and use them every day for You glory.
Teach me to be brave, to try new things,
and to never hide the light You gave me,
Show me how to use my talents to light,
and together we'll make the world
a better place.

What Is the Difference Between a Country and a Continent?

A **continent** is a huge piece of land on Earth. It is like a giant neighborhood that holds many different places.

There are 7 continents in the world: **Africa, Antarctica, Asia, Australia, Europe, North America,** and **South America.**

A **country** is a smaller place inside a continent. Each country has its own unique name, flag, people, language, and set of rules.

Think of it like this: A continent is like a big house, and countries are like different rooms inside that house.

Even though we live in different countries and continents, God made all children special, and we are all Heavenly Citizens

The Doctors at Home

Daddy and Mommy are my doctors at home,
When children feel sick, every heart finds its home.
From school or the hospital, we can't wait to go home
Because wherever we wander, our joy is back home.

They give us warm hugs when our little eyes roam,
They pray over us gently, in our safe, loving home.
With soups, smiles, and stories, they never leave us alone
God bless the doctors He placed in our home.

HEAVENLY CITIZEN

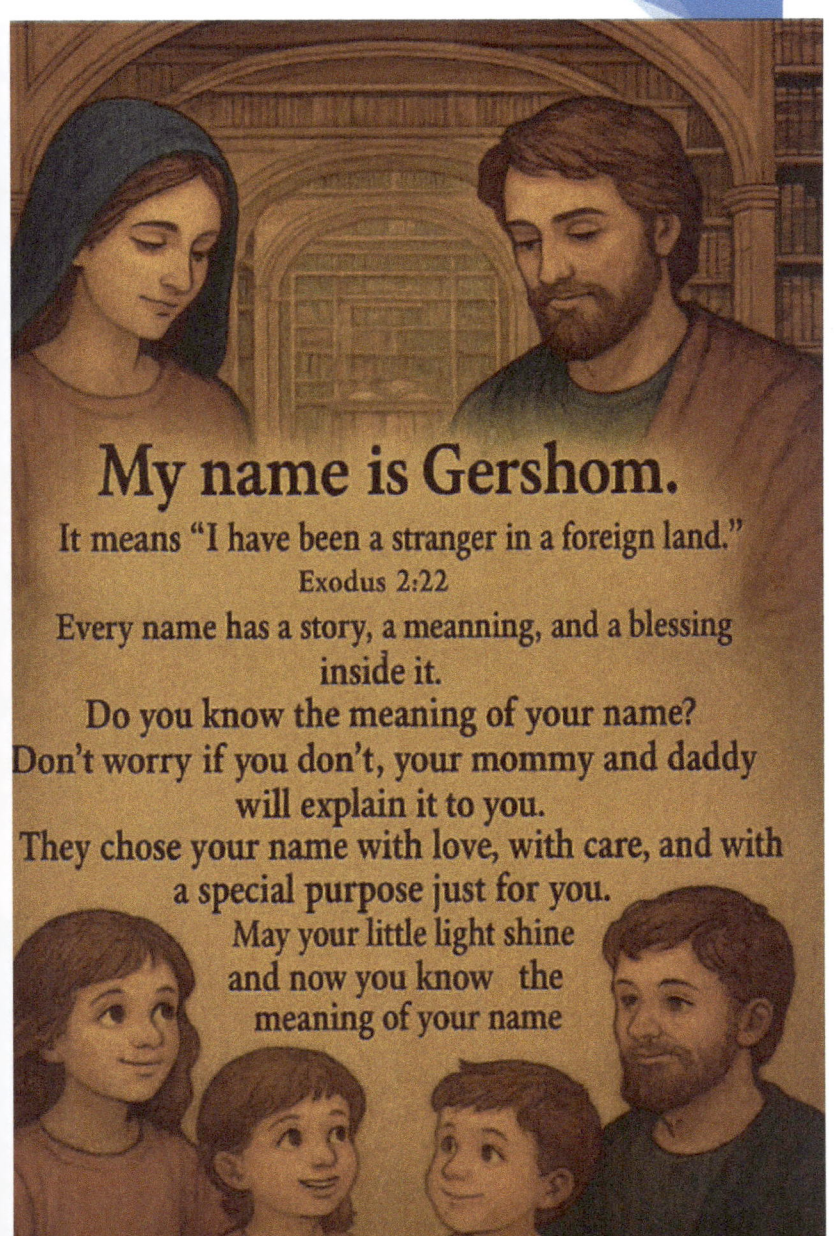

My name is Gershom.

It means "I have been a stranger in a foreign land."
Exodus 2:22

Every name has a story, a meanning, and a blessing inside it.
Do you know the meaning of your name?
Don't worry if you don't, your mommy and daddy will explain it to you.
They chose your name with love, with care, and with a special purpose just for you.
May your little light shine and now you know the meaning of your name

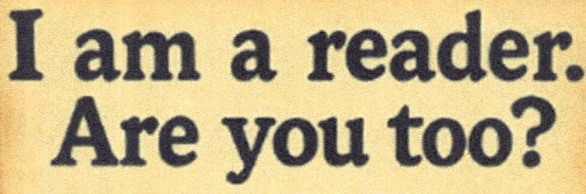

I am a reader. Are you too?

When I open a book, my mind becomes bright and alive. I learn new things, explore new places, and discover stories that make my heart grow. Reading makes me smarter, kinder, and braver every day. If you love books like I do, then you're a reader too—and readers can change the world!

I am a child of God and a citizen of the Kingdom of Heaven.

God created me with love, on purpose, and for a special reason. That means I belong to Him, and He watches over me wherever I go. I am part of His heavenly family, and His light shines in my heart. When I pray, obey, and show kindness, I live like a true citizen of the Kingdom of Heaven, a little light shining for God.

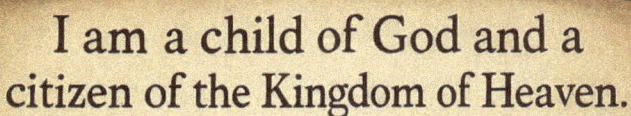

Do you know who Jesus is?

Jesus is the Son of God, the greatest friend that children can ever have. He loves every boy and girl in the whole world, and He watches over them day and night. Jesus came to teach us how to love, how to forgive, and how to be kind to others. He listens when we pray, He comforts us when we're sad, and He fills our hearts with light and peace. When you learn about Jesus, your heart becomes filled with love — Jesus is love.

1 John 4:8

My Love for Mommy and Daddy

Mommy and Daddy always tell me,
 "I love you" every day.
They hug me close; they keep me safe,
 In every little way.

Now it's my turn to say the words
 That make my heart feel true:
With smiles and giggles, arms open wide—
 Mommy, Daddy... I love you too.

You fill my world with joy and light,
 With kindness strong and steady.
So here I am with all my heart—
 My love is always ready.

I Love to Travel with My Family

Every trip feels like a new adventure!
Have you ever travelled before?
If not, don't worry, one day, your mommy ad daddy
will take you on a beautiful journey too.

When we travel, we start at an airport. There are big windows where you can watch airplanes take off and land. You can hear the engines roar and see people from all around the world.

Then comes the exciting part, getting on the airplane! We buckle our seatbelts, look out the window, and watch the world get smaller and smaller as we rise into tohe sky

Where do you dream of going one day?

Maybe a tropical beach, a snowy mountain, a big city, or a place where someone you love lives.

From one airport to another, every destination brings something new to learn, see, and enjoy.

Thank you, my friends.

Let me know which stories you liked the most!

Now you are smarter,
You are intelligent,
You are a reader,
You are a Heavenly Citizen,
You are a true Little Light for Jesus.
Let's shine and brighten the world together.

With love,
Gershom.

BUY A GIFT WITH GABRIEL'S OTHER BOOKS

My Children Are Friends with Jesus
Hardcover: 978-1-0696534-1-3
Paperback: 978-1-0696534-0-6
eBook: 978-1-0696240-8-3

The Book of Christian Men
Hardcover: 978-1-0696240-8-6
eBook: 978-1-06962240-7-9
eBook: 978-1-0696534-5-1

Mes Enfants Sont Amis Avec Jésus
Paperback: 978-1-0696554-4-4
Hardcover: 978-1-0696534-3-7
eBook: 978-1-0696534-2-0

Le Livre des Hommes Chrétiens
Hardcover: 978-1-0696240-2-4
Paperback: 978-1-0696240-1
eBook: 978-1-0696240-0-0

The Citizenship of Christian Parenthood
Hardcover: 978-1-0696240-2-4
Paperback: 978-1-0696240-1-7
eBook: 978-1-0696240-0-0

La Citoyenneté de la Parentalité Chrétienne
Hardcover: 978-1-0696240-5-5
Paperback: 978-1-0696240-4-8
eBook: 978-1-0696240-0-3-1

www.ingramcontent.com/pod-product-compliance
Lightning Source LLC
Chambersburg PA
CBHW061226070526
44584CB00029B/4009